# Christmas Carols
## for
## Solo Guitar

Arranged for Fingerstyle Guitar by Glenn Weiser

ISBN 1-57424-028-5
SAN 683-8022

Cover digital artwork - Shawn Brown
Music notation - Dave Celentano
Pasteup - Cindy Middlebrook

# Introduction

Both my parents sang in the church choir, so on Christmas Eve I always wound up with all the family around the piano singing the Yuletide carols. Mom handled the ivories and sang along with us kids while Dad played his old trombone. With the exception of Mom, it must have sounded god awful. But no matter; I loved the traditional music of Christmas from the start and still do.

In high school I studied classical guitar and later started teaching instrumental music. When the holiday season came around, I always made a point of arranging two or three carols for solo guitar. After a decade, there was enough material for a small book.

These arrangements vary in character. Some, like **It Came Upon A Midnight Clear**, use a fingerstyle guitar approach, while others, like **Hark! The Herald Angles Sing,** are close to the four-part choral versions. They are not too hard to play, and, I think, sound quite nice on guitar. Several of the songs are arranged with the dropped D tuning, so be sure to check the beginning of each song. If it is in dropped D look for the circle 6 -D.

So when the season arrives, tune up your instrument and let the warm sounds of Christmas fill the room.

Glenn Weiser

# About The Author

Glenn Weiser was born in Ridgewood, New Jersey in 1952 and began playing guitar at age 14. He studied classical guitar with Paul Battat and later ragtime fingerpicking with Eric Schoenberg. From there he went on to learn banjo, mandolin and harmonica. Glenn is the author of **Celtic Harp Music of Carolan & Others for Solo Guitar, Fiddle Tunes for Harmonica,** and **Blues and Rock Harmonica,** (Centerstream Publishing) plus **The Minstrel Boy** (Celtic Guitar Arrangements), **Christmas Carols For Two Guitars** (Cherry Lane). He has also written for Sing Out! magazine and Acoustic Guitar. Glenn currently teaches and performs in the Albany, New York area.

# CONTENTS

# Angels From The Realms Of Glory

arr. by G. Weiser

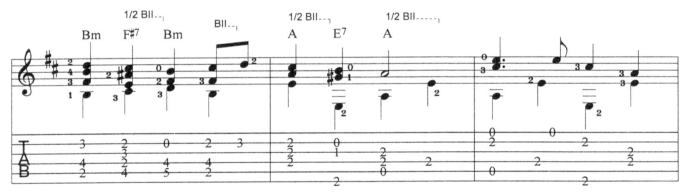

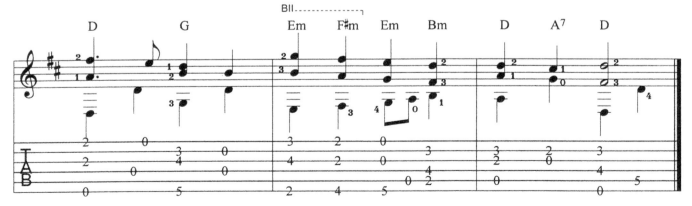

# Away In A Manger

arr. by G. Weiser

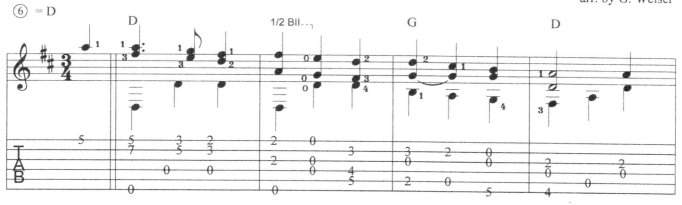

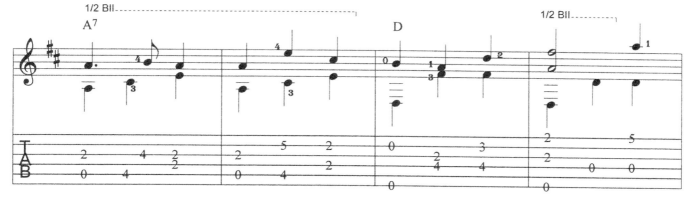

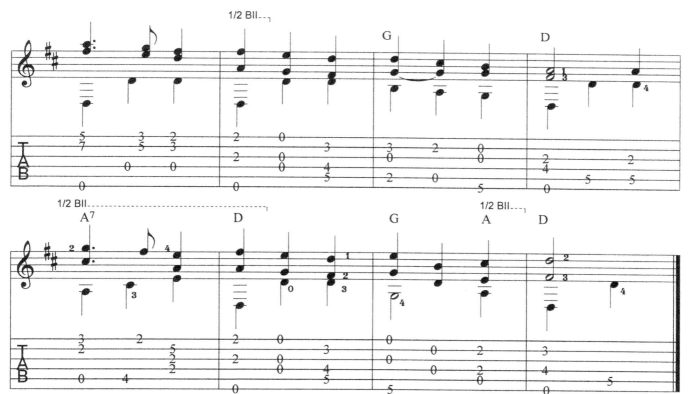

# Deck The Halls

arr. by G. Weiser

# The First Noel

arr. by G. Weiser

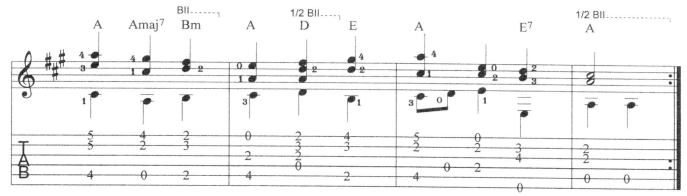

# God Rest Ye Merry Gentlemen

arr. by G. Weiser

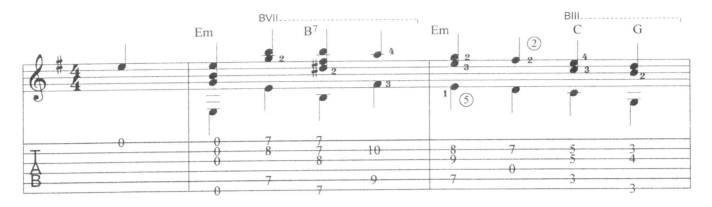

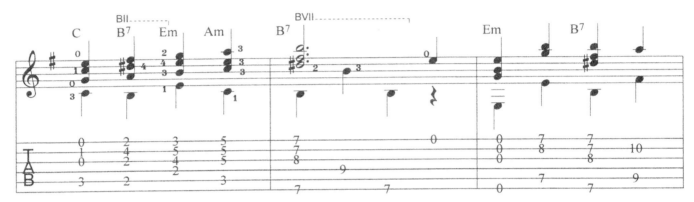

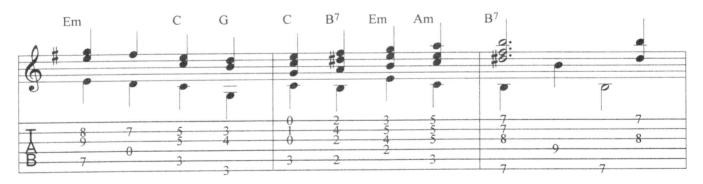

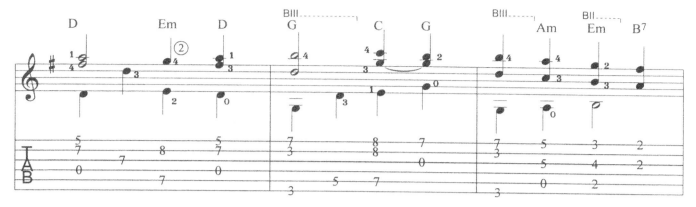

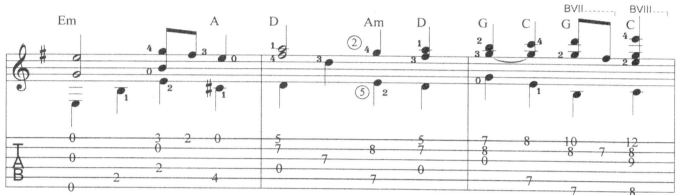

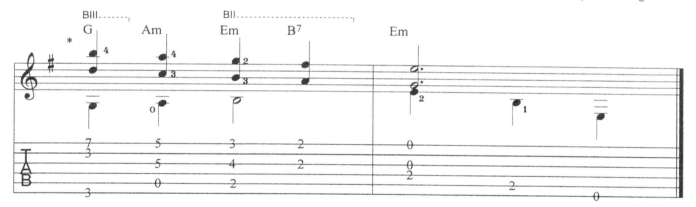

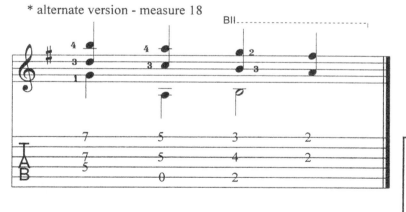

* alternate version - measure 18

**New words for the modern days**

God rest ye merry gentlemen
Let nothing you dismay.

For if you work and fret all day
Why then you are Type A.

And if you cannot calm your ire
Your heart it will give way:

Refrain:
  Oh Type B, you must be Type B-Be Type B,
  Oh Type B, you must be Type B.

-Dedicated to John Hill-

# Good King Wenceslas

arr. by G. Weiser

⑥ = D

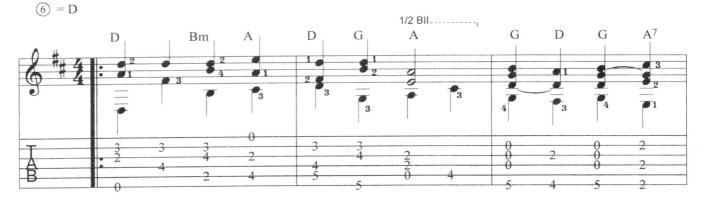

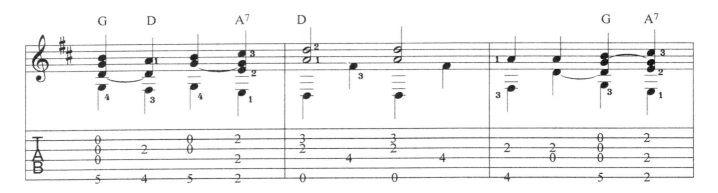

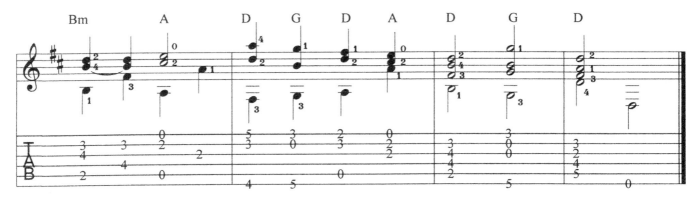

# Hark! The Herald Angels Sing

arr. by G. Weiser

⑥ = D

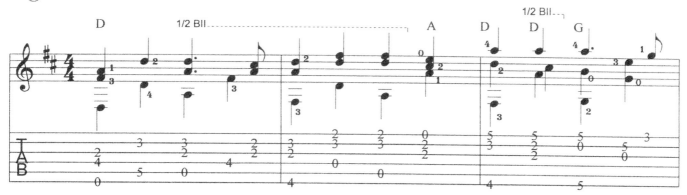

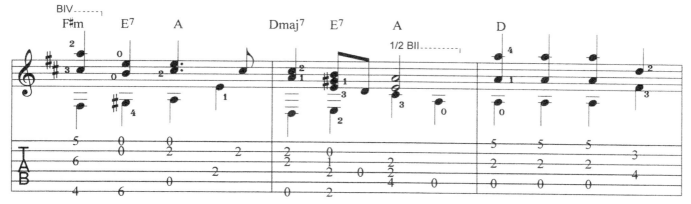

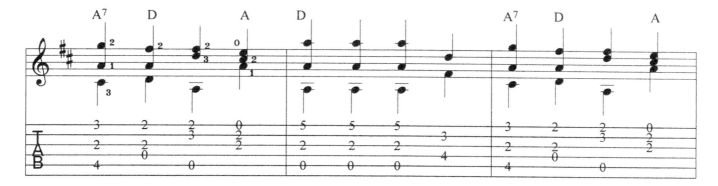

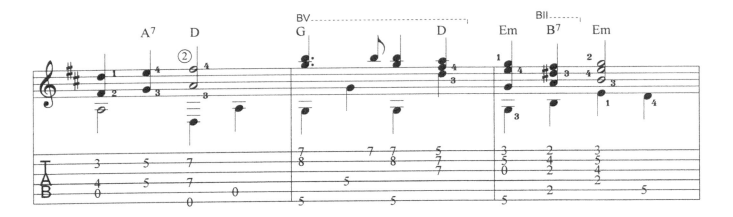

# Hearken, All! What Holy Singing

⑥ = D

arr. by G. Weiser

# The Holly And The Ivy

arr. by G. Weiser

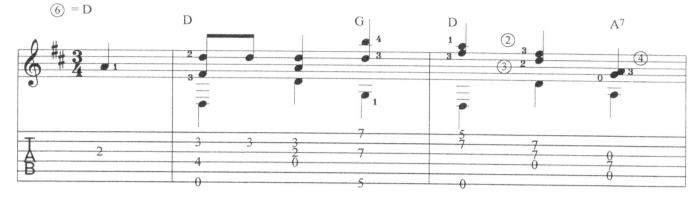

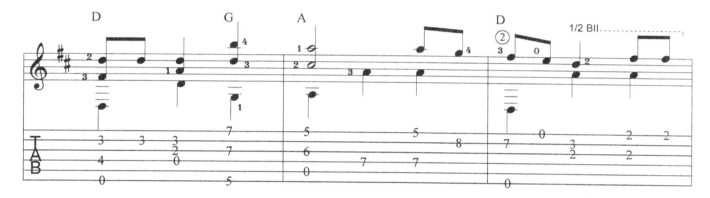

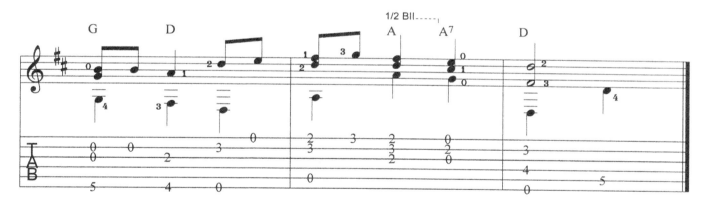

HOW LONG TO KEEP THE CHRISTMAS TREE: A VISUAL GUIDE

# I Saw Three Ships

## (First Air)

arr. by G. Weiser

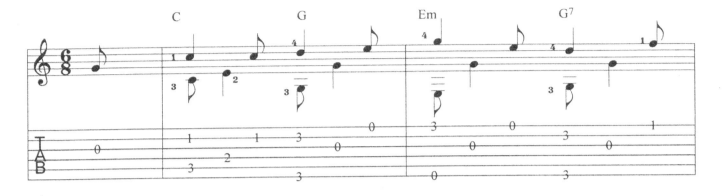

# I Saw Three Ships

*(Second Air)*

arr. by G. Weiser

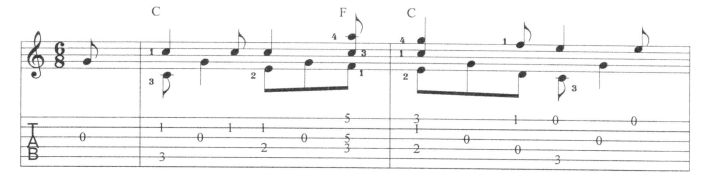

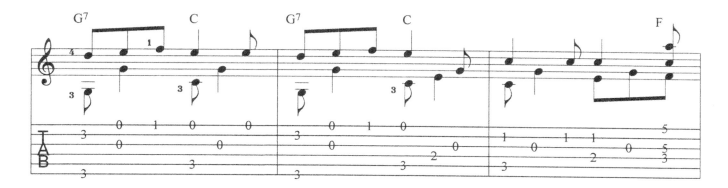

# Joy To The World

arr. by G. Weiser

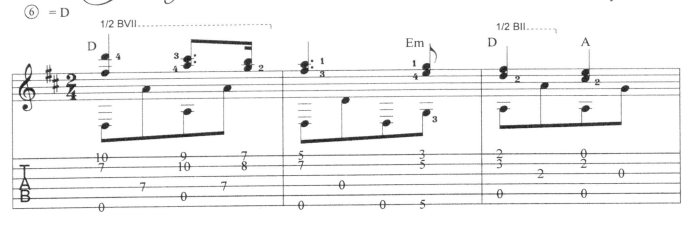

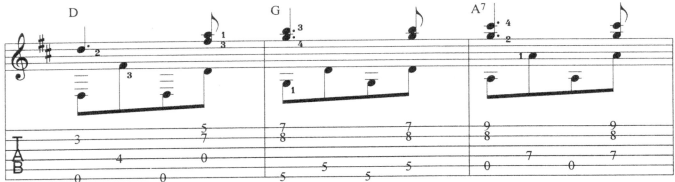

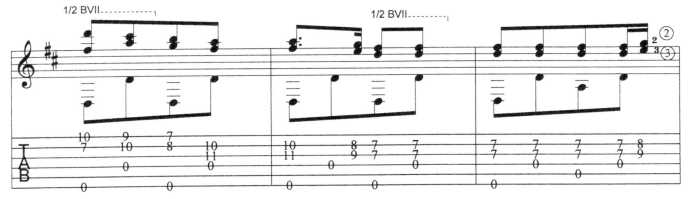

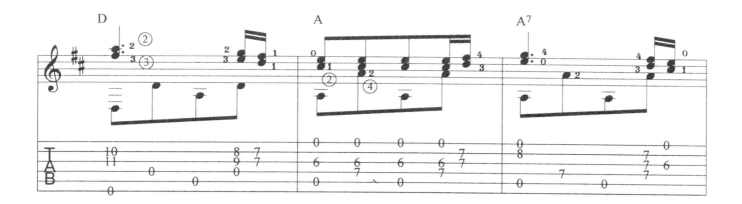

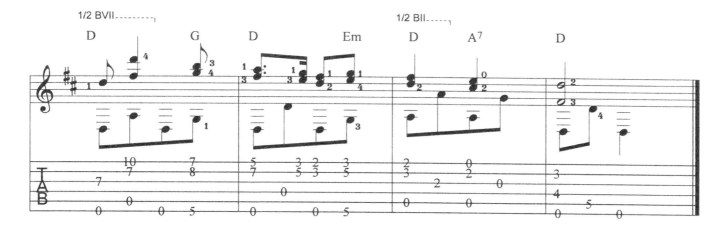

## Yule-Tide Folk Charms

According to ancient traditions in many lands, Christmas is the time when magical charms work best. Listed below are a few old customs that you might want to revive this year. They may not bring you health, happiness, and prosperity, but a few are guaranteed to bring you notoriety in your neighborhood.

- Beat the fruit trees with a green switch on Christmas night, and they will bear more fruit the following year.
- On Christmas Eve thrash the garden with a flail (a hand thrashing tool), wearing only a shirt, and the crops will grow well the next year.
- On Christmas day hang a wash cloth on a hedge, then groom the horses with it to make them grow fat.
- Burn elder on Christmas Eve and all the witches and sorcerers of the neighborhood will be revealed to you.
- Carry nothing forth from the house on Christmas day until something has been brought in order to avoid bad luck.
- Steal some hay the night before Christmas and give it the cattle. They will thrive, and you will not be caught in any thefts for a whole year.
- All who help to bring in the Yule log will be protected from witchcraft the following year.
- Save a piece of the Yule log and keep it under the bed to protect the house from fire and lighting.
- Hang mistletoe over the door of the byre (cow barn) to protect the cattle from disease.
- Wear something sewed with thread spun on Christmas Eve and no vermin will stick to you.

# Lo, How A Rose E'er Blooming

arr. by G. Weiser

# O Christmas Tree

arr. by G. Weiser

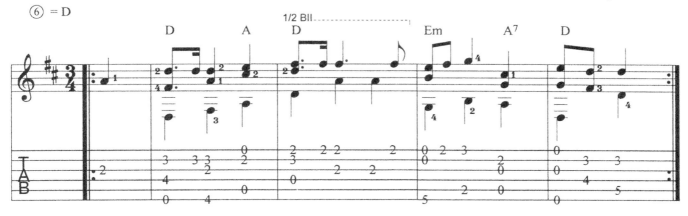

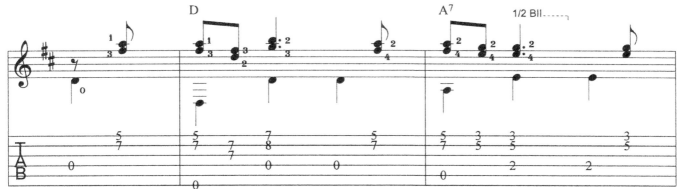

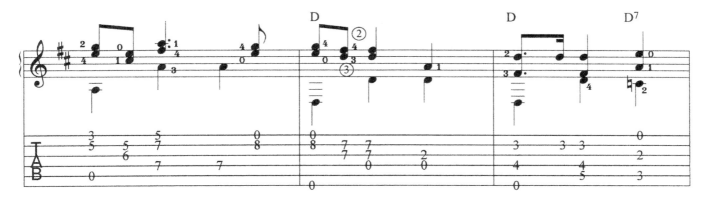

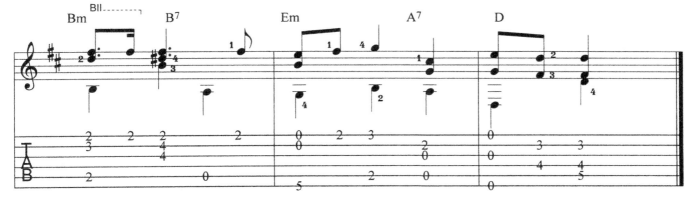

# O Come, All Ye Faithful

arr. by G. Weiser

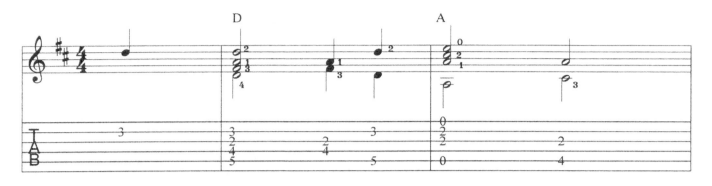

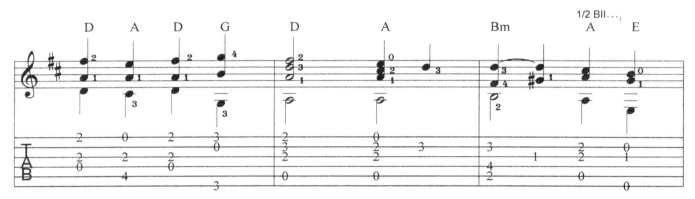

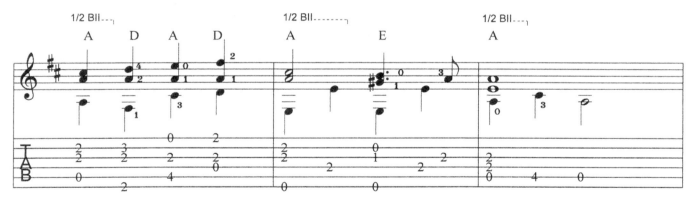

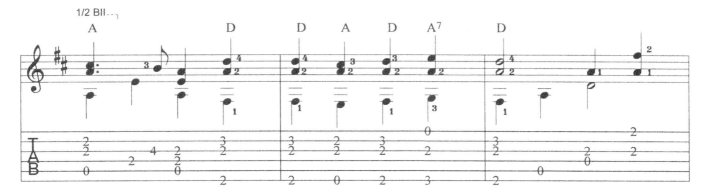

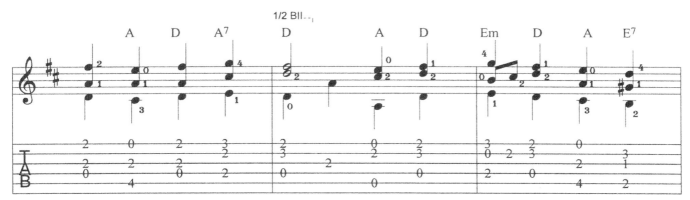

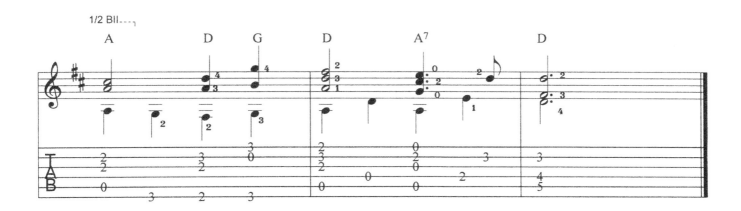

# O Come, O Come, Emanuel

arr. by G. Weiser

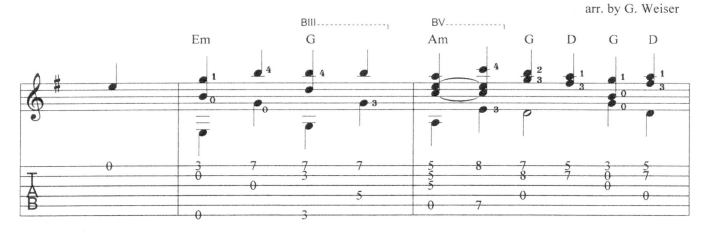

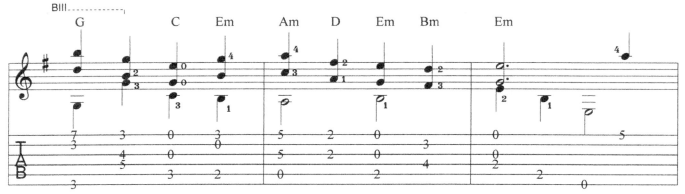

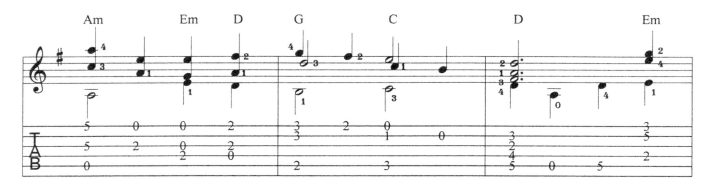

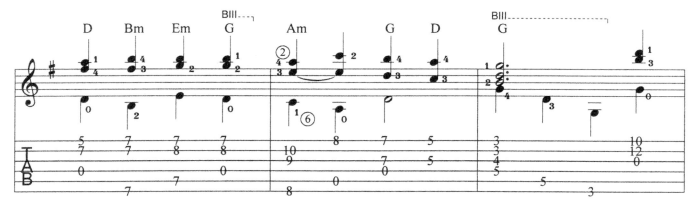

San Francisco, 1891

# The Origin of Christmas Kettles

The Salvation Army Captain in San Francisco had resolved, in December of 1891, to provide a free Christmas dinner to the area's poor persons. But how would he pay for the food?

As he went about his daily tasks, the question stayed in his mind. Suddenly, his thoughts went back to his days as a sailor in Liverpool, England. On the Stage Landing he saw a large pot. Called "Simpson's pot" into which charitable donations were thrown by passersby.

On the next morning, he secured permission from the authorities to place a similar pot at the Oakland ferry landing, at the foot of Market Street. No time was lost in securing the pot and placing it in a conspicuous position, so that it could be seen by all those going to and from the ferry boats. In addition, a brass urn was placed on a stand in the waiting room for the same purpose.

Thus, Captain Joseph McFee launched a tradition that has spread not only throughout the United States, but throughout the world.

In 1897, McIntyre prepared his Christmas plans for Boston around the kettle, but his fellow officers refused to cooperate for fear of "making spectacles of themselves." So McIntyre, his wife and his sister set up three kettles at the Washington Street thoroughfare in the heart of the city. That year the kettle effort in Boston and other locations nationwide resulted in 150,000 Christmas dinners for the needy.

In 1898, the *New York World* newspaper hailed The Salvation Army kettles as "the newest and most novel device for collecting money."

Some of the new kettles have such devices as a self-ringing bell and a booth complete with public address system over which the traditional Christmas carols are broadcast.

# O Little Town Of Bethlehem

arr. by G. Weiser

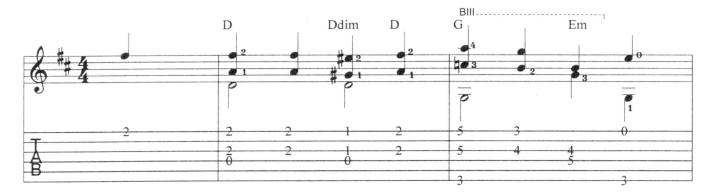

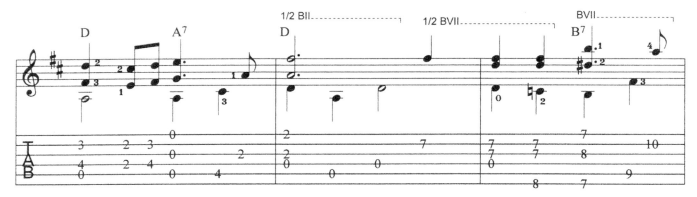

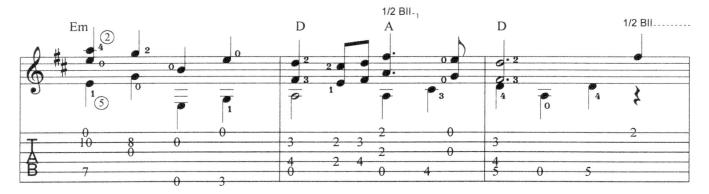

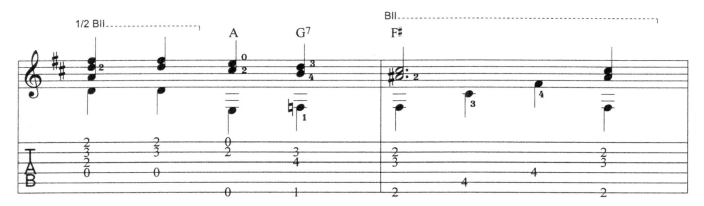

## Holiday Traditions

The Christmas season in <u>Mexico</u> last from December 16 to January 6. Traditionally, a play called a Posada is performed on the nine evenings before Christmas Day. This Posada is acted out by members of the family and is symbolic of Mary and Joseph's search for a room on Christmas Eve. Usually, there is a social hour after each Posada at which gifts and candy are exchanged.

Should you find yourself in one of the <u>South American</u> countries on the eve of Epiphany, the twelfth day after Christmas, be certain to leave water and hay on your doorstep. This will insure that on this night, the wise Men's camels have plenty of food and water as they travel forth.

And, if you happen to be single, be careful about standing in church doorways in <u>Switzerland</u> on Christmas Eve. Legend has it thereabouts that if young people visit nine fountains on their way to midnight church services and take three sips of water from each, they will meet their future spouse at the church door.

In <u>Yugoslavia</u>, the children really have it made. The second Sunday before Christmas is known as Mother's Day. On this day, while mom is sitting quietly, the kids sneak in and tie her feet to her chair. Then they shout, "Mother's Day, Mother's Day, what will you pay to get away?" Under the circumstances, mom is more than happy to give the kids a few gifts. And, since they've got a successful racket going, what do you think happens the next Sunday? Right. This time it's dad that gets the treatment - and, like mom, he caves in under the pressure.

Jolly old <u>England</u> Celebrates Boxing Day. It's the name given to the day after Christmas where it's customary to give money to all the people who have served you throughout the year. This usually includes milkmen, postmen and paper boys.

Throughout the world you can find a variety of unique customs and traditions, but running through all of them is a common thread. It is a thread of love, a wish for peace on earth and a feeling of goodwill toward all.

# Silent Night

arr. by G. Weiser

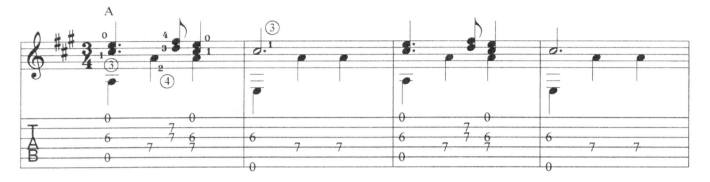

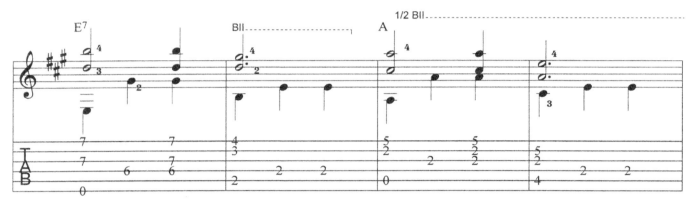

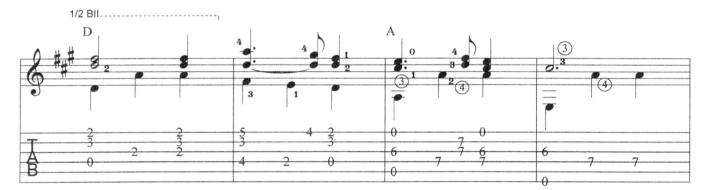

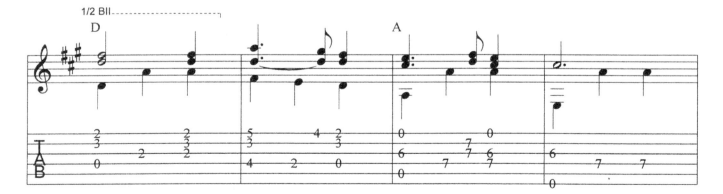

28

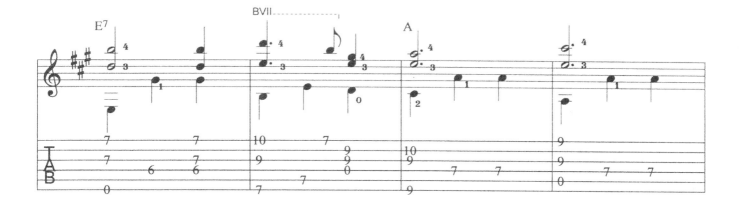

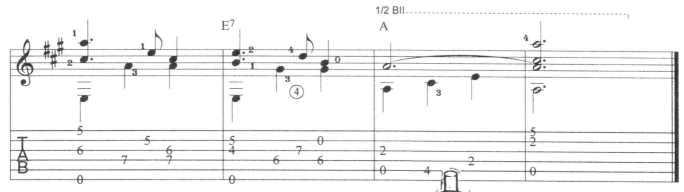

29

# The Twelve Days Of Christmas

arr. by G. Weiser

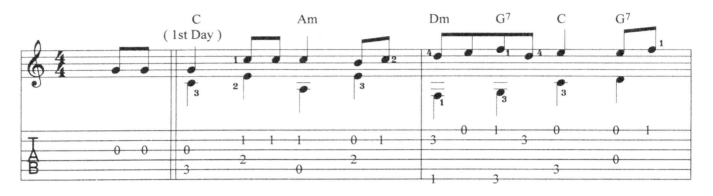

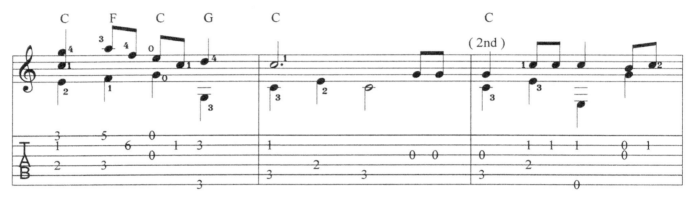

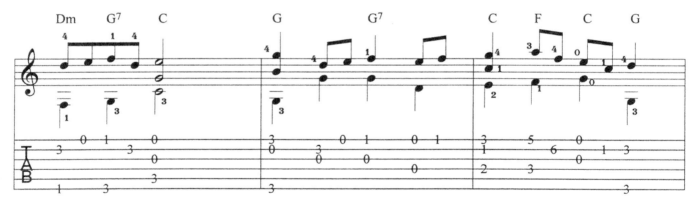

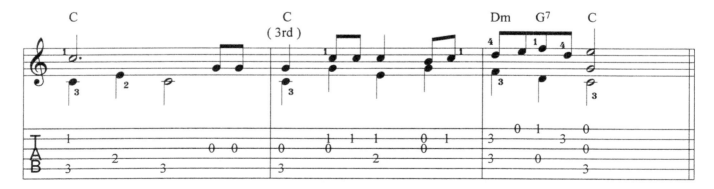

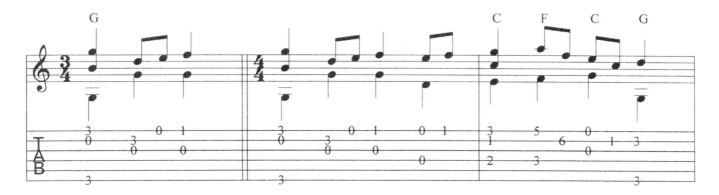

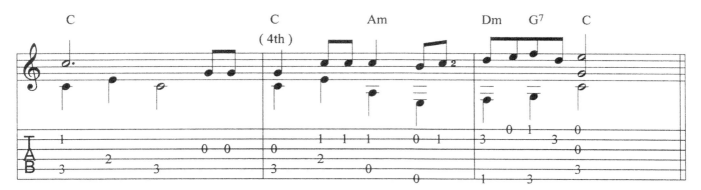

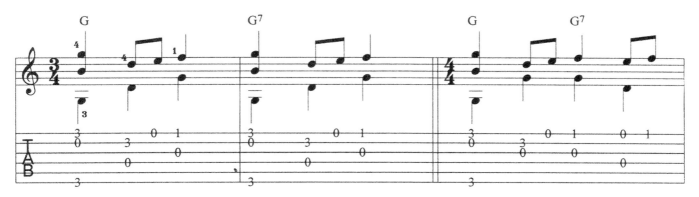

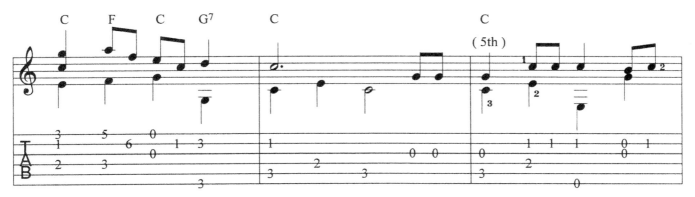

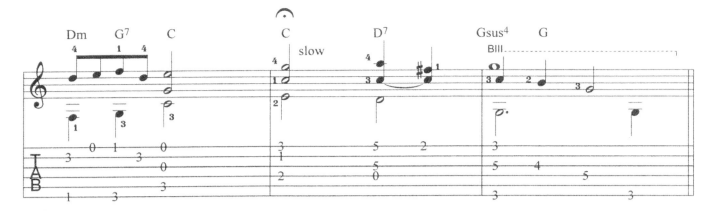

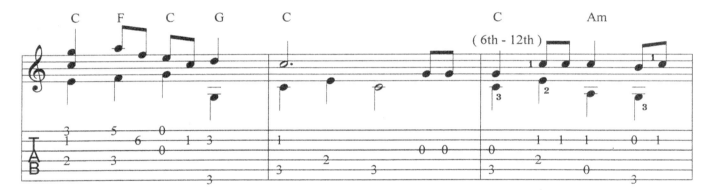

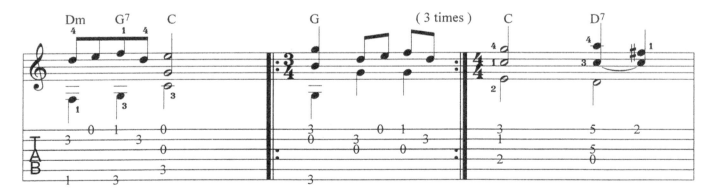

32

## Holiday Traditions

In <u>Italy</u>, children receive their gifts on the sixth of January. Their presents are said to be delivered by an old woman wearing a raincoat, long dress and a scarf. She is called the Befana. Like a witch, the Befana travels through the night on a broom (instead of a sleigh and eight reindeer) bringing presents to good Italian children. The highlight of Christmas in Rome is midnight Mass on Christmas Eve celebrated by the Pope in St. Peter's Basilica.

In <u>France</u>, children put their shoes on the doorstep on Christmas Eve so "Le Petit Noel" (the Christ Child) can fill them with gifts. The French use mistletoe as a symbol of good luck during the holiday season. In France's southern region of Provence, tradition calls for the entire family to carry a Yule log, which must be big enough to burn from Christmas to New Year's Day, into the home. French families often set up a small nativity scene and enjoy Strasbourg pie and black pudding during the Christmas festivities.

In <u>China</u> and <u>Japan</u> Christians observe customs that are similar to those in the United States. The Chinese call their Santa Claus "Sheng Tan Lao Ren," which means Holy Birthday Old Man.

In <u>Norway</u>, the Yuletide season starts on St. Thomas' Day, December 21. Norwegians bake cakes especially for St. Thomas on Christmas Eve. Another Norwegian custom is to "ringe in Julen" (ring in Christmas). Church bells throughout the country are rung at 4pm on Christmas Eve as a symbol of welcoming the holiday. Norwegians prepare a traditional pudding containing a single almond. It is believed that the person who gets the almond will be the next to get married.

# We Three Kings

arr. by G. Weiser

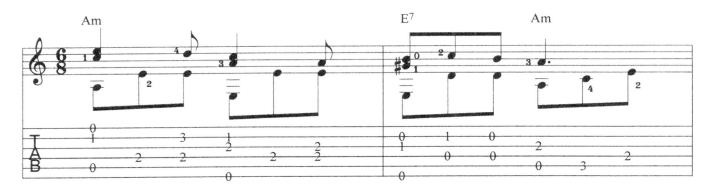

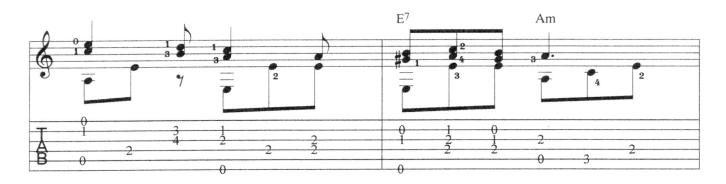

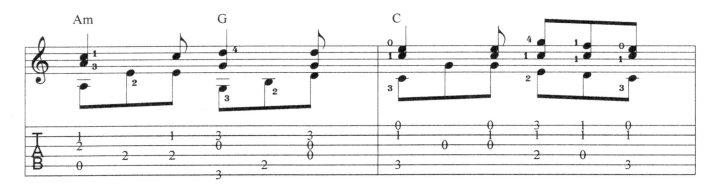

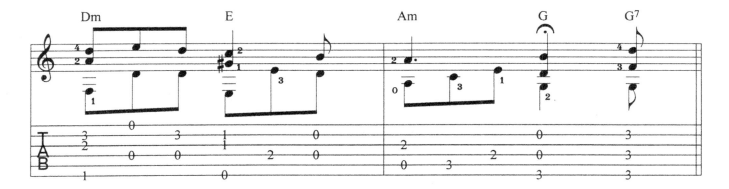

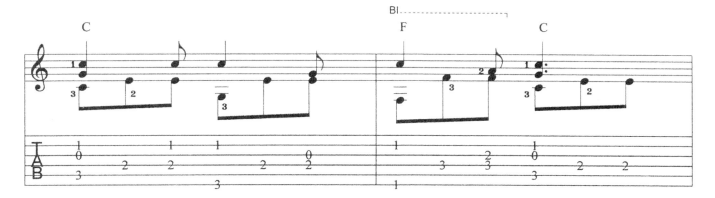

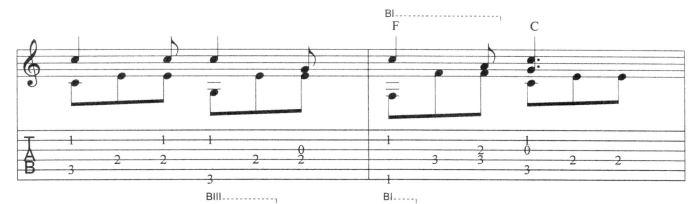

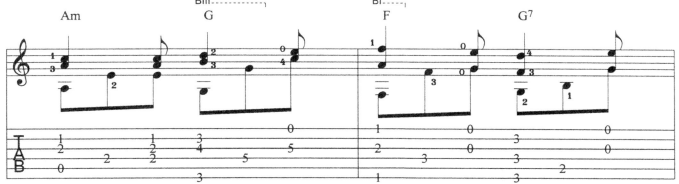

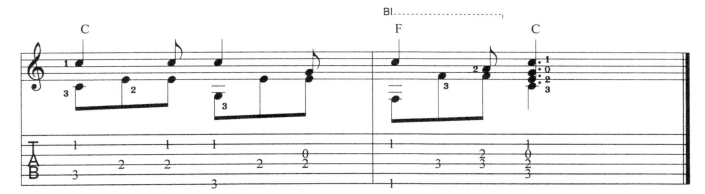

# We Wish You A Merry Christmas

arr. by G. Weiser

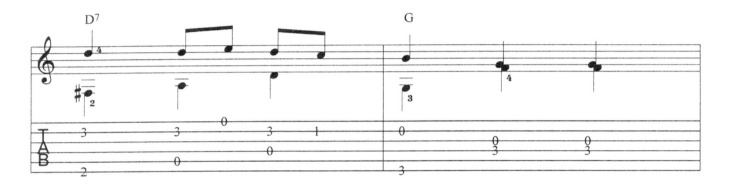

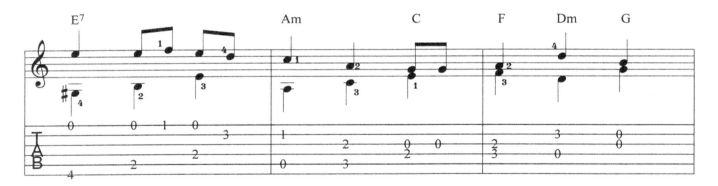

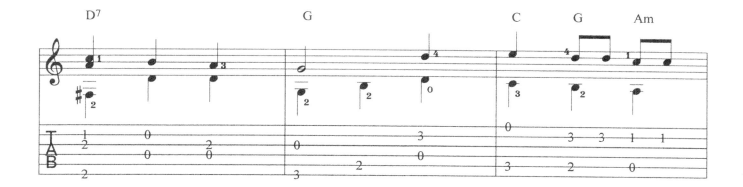

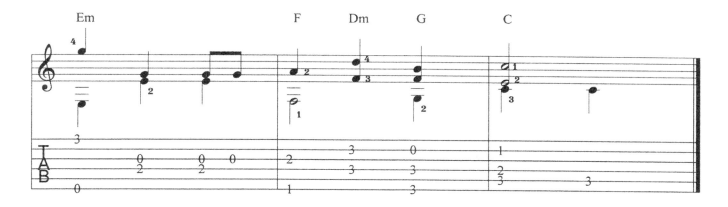

*
alternate harmony
measures 10 - 12

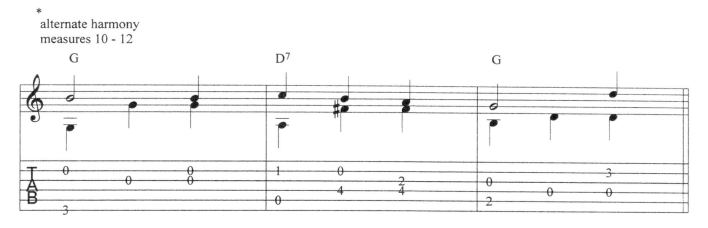

# What Child Is This?

arr. by G. Weiser

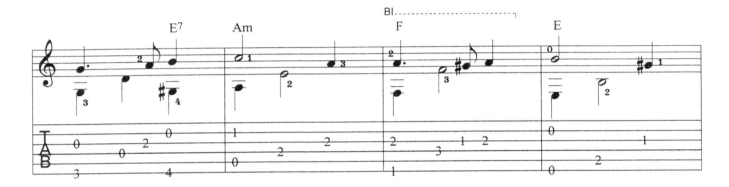

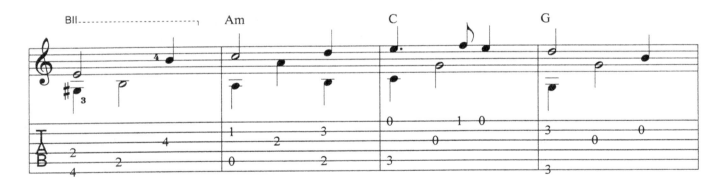

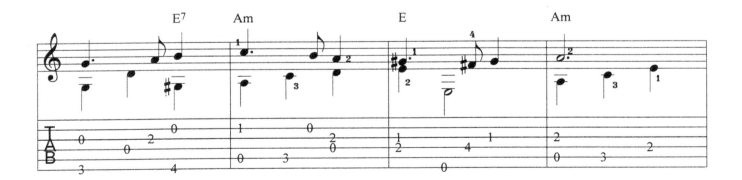

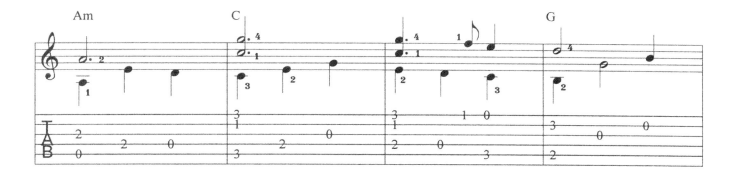

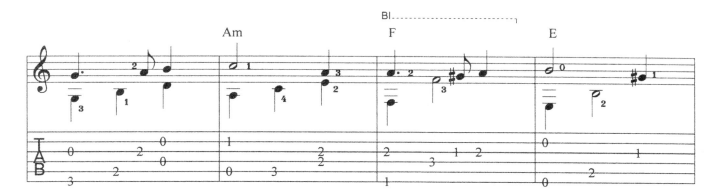

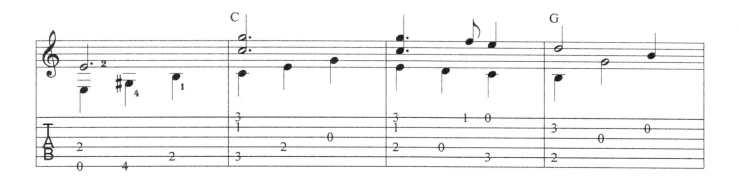

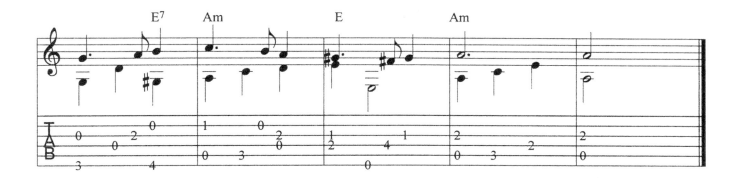